GARAGE STORAGE

We ask a lot of our garages. We use them as a place to do home projects and we store lots of stuff in them. And oh yeah, we'd like to park our cars in there too, though all too often the garage is so filled with tools, recreational equipment, extra furniture, and so on that the auto is relegated to the driveway.

The key to a successfully multitasking garage is to get the stuff off the floor, and this Quick Guide offers easy-to-build projects to help you do just that. You'll find sturdy utility shelves, a generous overhead unit, a simple wall rack for garden tools, and a fold-up worktable/cabinet. Welcome back, family auto!

UTILITY SHELVES

Looking for sturdy shelving that's inexpensive and quick and easy to build? All you need is a pile of 2×4s and a sheet of CDX plywood—a sturdy grade of plywood that's most commonly used for house sheathing. The shelves are 48 in. long to make efficient use of the plywood sheet. You can easily adapt the plan to fit your space by making the unit shorter or changing the depth of the shelves. And if you have lots of stuff to store, it won't take much more time to assemble two or three of these while you are at it.

WHAT YOU'LL NEED

• 5 shelves	¾ in. × 16 in. × 48 in.
• 10 long rails	1½ in. × 1½ in. × 48 in.
• 10 side rails	1½ in. × 1½ in. × 13 in.
• 4 stiles	1½ in. × 3½ in. × 77 in.
• 4 bottom spacers	1½ in. × 3½ in. × 6 in.
• 16 spacers	1½ in. × 3½ in. × 15 in.

HARDWARE

• 2½-in. all-purpose screws

• 1¼-in. all-purpose screws

QUICK TIP If you are making more than one shelving unit, save time by cutting parts for all the units at one time.

Cutting Drawing for Ten 8-ft. 2×4s

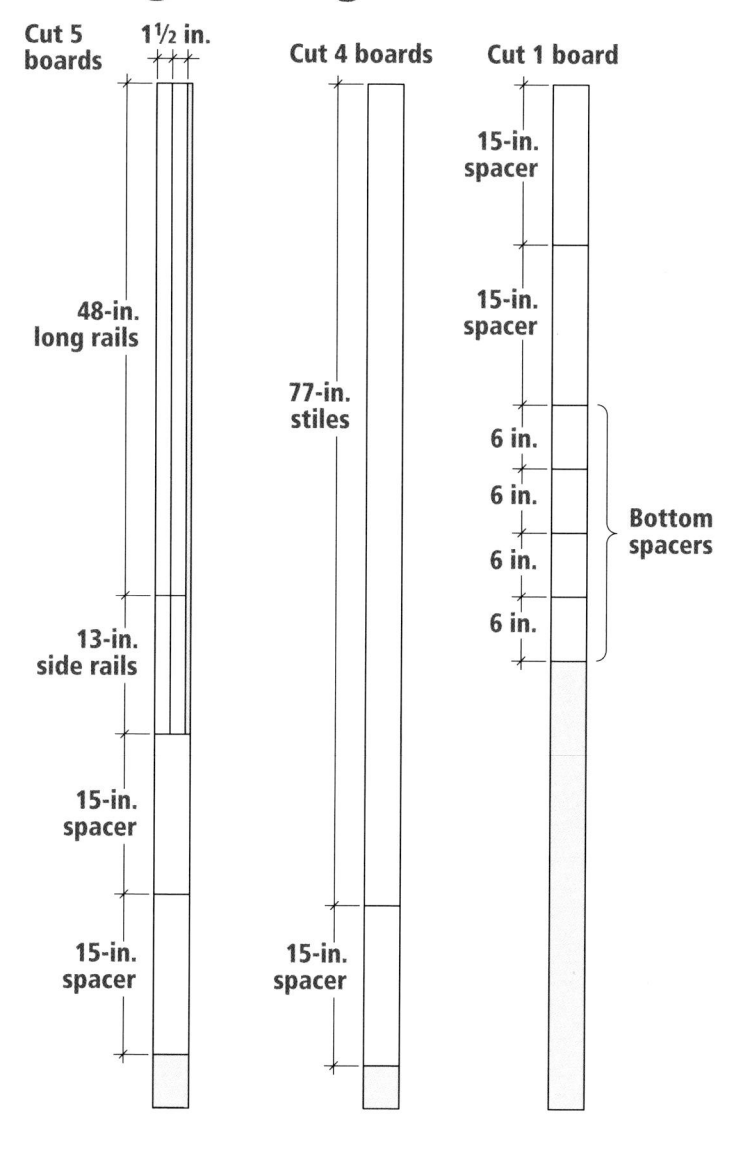

Cut 5 boards

1½ in.

48-in. long rails

13-in. side rails

15-in. spacer

15-in. spacer

Cut 4 boards

77-in. stiles

15-in. spacer

Cut 1 board

15-in. spacer

15-in. spacer

6 in.

6 in.

6 in.

6 in.

Bottom spacers

Front View

Side View

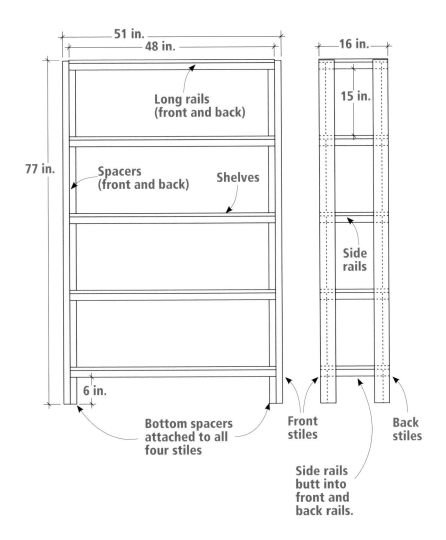

Front View

51 in.

48 in.

77 in.

Long rails
(front and back)

Spacers
(front and back)

Shelves

6 in.

Bottom spacers
attached to all
four stiles

Side View

16 in.

15 in.

Side
rails

Front
stiles

Back
stiles

Side rails
butt into
front and
back rails.

CUT THE PARTS

1. CUT THE PLYWOOD. Put the plywood for the shelves on the floor with scraps of plywood underneath and lay out the first crosscut at 16 in. Set the blade on your circular saw to cut through the plywood and into the scrap without cutting into the floor. Lay out and cut the rest of the shelves.

2. CROSSCUT THE LUMBER PARTS TO LENGTH. The cutting drawing on p. 3 shows how to get all the parts from ten 8-ft. 2×4s. First, make all the crosscuts. When cutting four or five boards to the same length, clamp them together flush at the ends and make each cut in one pass.

3. RIP THE RAILS TO WIDTH. Use a tablesaw to rip all the 48-in. pieces and all the 13-in. pieces into 1½-in. by 1½-in. rails. Be sure to use a push stick when making these cuts.

> **QUICK TIP** If you don't have a tablesaw to rip the rails, you can purchase 8-ft. 2×2s (actual size 1½ in. by 1½ in.) at a lumberyard or home center.

ASSEMBLE THE UNIT

1. ATTACH THE BOTTOM SPACERS. All the lumber connections are made with 2½-in. screws. Attach a bottom spacer to each stile with two screws. Use a clamp to help hold the spacer in position while you drive the screws.

2. ATTACH A LONG RAIL. Place two stiles on edge and position a long rail between. Attach with two screws on each end—one through the stile and one into the bottom spacer.

3. ATTACH A SIDE RAIL. Put a side rail in place butting into the long rail and secure it with one screw through the stile and one into the bottom spacer.

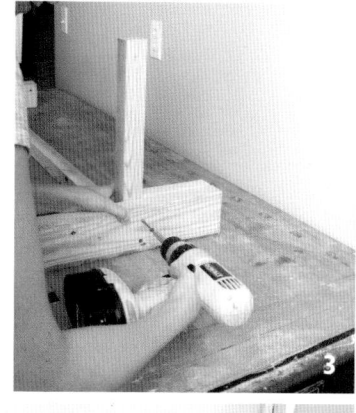

4. ADD THE SECOND BOTTOM RAILS. Stand up the stile/rail assembly you made and clamp it to the side of your workbench, or have a helper hold it upright. Put the other two stiles and a long rail in place. Screw the side rails to the bottom spacers and stiles.

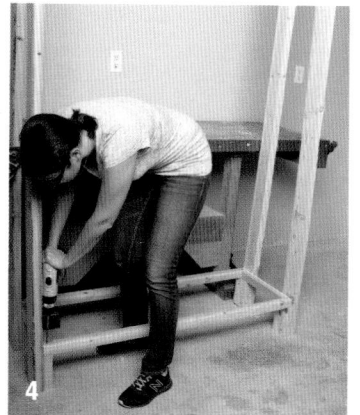

5. INSTALL THE LOWEST SHELF. Put a shelf in place and attach it to the rails with 1¼-in. screws spaced about every 6 in.

> **QUICK TIP**
> When securing a 1½-in. by 1½-in. rail to a spacer, predrill the hole to prevent splitting the end of the rail. You may want to predrill all the holes for the 2½-in. screws, just to make it easier to drive them. To select the right size drill bit, hold the screw behind the bit—if you can see the screw threads but not the body of the screw, you have the right bit.

6. ADD SPACERS AND COMPLETE THE UNIT. At each corner, put a spacer down against the shelf and secure it to the stiles with four 2½-in. screws. Repeat the process for adding rails, shelves, and spacers until the unit is complete.

Commercial Wall-Storage Systems

Getting stuff off the floor and up on the wall is an essential part of any garage storage scheme. There are lots of wall systems you can buy to help you achieve this goal. You'll find hooks designed to hold various items—from garden hoses to garden tools to bicycles or ladders. There are metal grids to which you attach various hooks, baskets, and shelves at different heights.

If you want the option of easily changing your wall storage layout, channels are a great way to go because hooks, baskets, and shelves can be snapped in or removed in seconds. Some channel systems are designed to cover whole walls. Or you can purchase individual lengths of channel. The channel system shown here uses 48-in.-long channels. The end caps are sold separately, so you can line up the channels for lengths in any 48-in. increment. You screw the channels into studs, and then you snap in the accessories of your choice.

OVERHEAD GARAGE STORAGE

This storage rack, constructed of 2×4s and plywood, is a great way to gain storage while sacrificing zero floor space. It is extremely sturdy thanks to the use of lag screws, joist hangers, and L-angles.

The simple design is easily adapted to many garage situations. The 30-in.-deep version shown here is installed in a garage with a 10-ft. ceiling, leaving plenty of room to walk beneath. If your ceiling is lower, you can make a shallower unit, or you can reduce the width or length to suit as long as you space the joists 4 ft. or less on center.

Overhead Storage

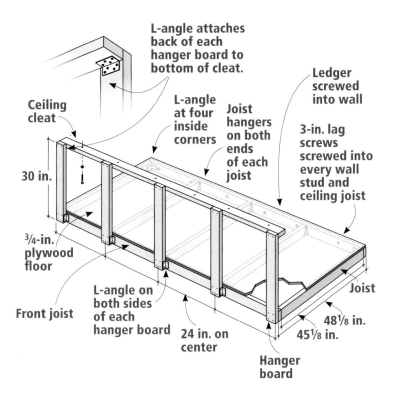

L-angle attaches back of each hanger board to bottom of cleat.

Ceiling cleat

L-angle at four inside corners

Joist hangers on both ends of each joist

Ledger screwed into wall

3-in. lag screws screwed into every wall stud and ceiling joist

30 in.

¾-in. plywood floor

Front joist

L-angle on both sides of each hanger board

24 in. on center

Hanger board

48⅛ in.

45⅛ in.

Joist

WHAT YOU'LL NEED

• 1 ledger	1½ in. × 3½ in. × 8 ft.
• 1 front joist	1½ in. × 3½ in. × 8 ft.
• 1 ceiling cleat	1½ in. × 3½ in. × 8 ft.
• 5 hanger boards	1½ in. × 3½ in. × 30 in.
• 5 joists	1½ in. × 3½ in. × 45⅛ in.
• 1 floor	¾ in. × 4 ft. × 8 ft. CDX plywood

HARDWARE

- 12 lag screws, ¼ in. dia. × 3 in.
- 2½-in. all-purpose screws
- 17 L-angles for 2×4 construction
- 6 joist hangers for 2×4s
- 1½-in. joist hanger nails
- 1¼-in. all-purpose screws

QUICK TIP A full sheet of plywood is used for the floor of this overhead storage rack. If you don't have a way to transport 4-ft.-wide sheets, have the lumberyard or home center cut the sheet in half along its length. The seam won't matter in the finished project.

1. LAY OUT JOIST AND HANGER BOARD POSITIONS. Clamp three 8-ft. 2×4s together, edges up and ends flush. Starting from your left, strike lines at 23¼ in., 47¼ in., and 71¼ in. Make an X to the right of each line. On two of those boards, extend the lines and Xs to one face; label these boards as the ledger and the front joist. Extend the lines to the other face of the front joist. Label the third board as the ceiling cleat.

2. LAY OUT THE LEDGER. Use a 4-ft. level to draw an 8-ft.-long level line along the wall 30 in. from the ceiling.

3. FIND THE STUDS ALONG THE LINE. If your garage isn't painted, you can easily identify stud locations by the vertical rows of nails or screws. Otherwise, use a stud finder to mark where your layout line crosses each stud.

3

4   5

5. SECURE THE LEDGER. Predrill and install one lag screw with washer into each stud along the length of the ledger. If a screw falls over an X, you'll need to counterbore the screw hole so the screw head will be below the surface where it won't interfere with the joist. Make the counterbore with a 3/4-in. spade bit, then predrill the screw hole through the counterbore.

4. POSITION THE LEDGER. With a helper holding one end, align the bottom of the ledger to the layout line with the X marks to your left. Drive a 2 1/2-in. screw through the ledger into the stud closest to one end of the board. Check for level, and then drive a screw into the stud closest to the other end.

6. LAY OUT THE CEILING CLEAT. Use a 4-ft. level to make a plumb mark on the ceiling above each end of the ledger. Use a framing square to make a line on the ceiling square to each end. Then use a chalkline to extend these lines 48⅛ in. from each end. (That extra ⅛ in. will make it easier to slide the plywood floor into place.) Snap a line parallel to the wall between the ends of the two lines. Use a stud finder to mark where the line crosses joists in the ceiling.

What if the Joists Run Parallel to the Ceiling Cleat?

This project assumes that the ceiling joists in your garage run perpendicular to the ceiling cleat. If the joists run parallel to the cleat, you have two choices: You can adjust the width of the storage unit to the nearest joist. Or you can make five 2×4 cross-cleats to span two joists. Use 3-in. lag screws to attach the cross-cleats through the ceiling into the joists. Then lag-screw the ceiling cleat to the cross-cleats.

7. INSTALL THE CEILING CLEAT. With a helper, align the ceiling cleat to the inside of the line, with the Xs to your right as you face the wall. Hold the cleat in place with a screw into a joist at each end. Predrill, and then install one lag screw into each joist.

8. CUT AND INSTALL THE HANGER BOARDS. Using a circular saw or power miter saw, cut the five hanger boards to length. Position each along its layout line, covering the X and butting into the ceiling, then attach it to the cleat with a 2½-in. screw. Check for plumb, and then add a second screw.

9. INSTALL L-ANGLES WHERE CLEAT MEETS HANGERS. Use an L-angle with 1¼-in. screws to attach the back face of each hanger board to the bottom of the ceiling cleat.

10. INSTALL THE JOIST HANGERS.

Using 1½-in. joist hanger nails, install three joist hangers on the ledger and three on the front joist positioned so that the joist ends will cover the X at the three inner layout lines. It's important to install the hangers before you install the front joist because the hanger boards are not yet stable enough to hammer against. Use a scrap of 2×4 as shown to make sure the hangers are properly positioned.

10

11

12

11. INSTALL THE OUTER L-ANGLES.

Strike a line 1½ in. from each end of the ledger (the thickness of each joist) and the front joist. Install an L-angle at each end of the ledger and the front joist.

12. POSITION THE FRONT JOIST.

With a helper, align both ends of the front joist to the bottom outside edges of the outermost hanger joists and then clamp the joist in place.

13. ATTACH THE FRONT JOIST. Clamp the front joist to another hanger board. Check that the front joist is level and then make the connection with four 2½-in. screws. Clamp and then screw each connection.

14. INSTALL THE JOISTS. Cut the five joists to 45⅛ in. long. Then slip three of the joists into their joist hangers and secure them with 1½-in. joist hanger nails into the angled hole on each side of each joist hanger. Put the outer joists against the L-angles and secure with 1¼-in. screws.

15. INSTALL THE REMAINING L-ANGLES. Use L-angles and 1¼-in. screws to secure each side of each hanger board to the front joist.

16. INSTALL THE FLOOR. Put the plywood in place, climb aboard, and snap lines to locate the joists below at 24 in., 48 in., and 72 in. Secure the plywood with 1¼-in. screws about every 12 in. into the ledger, front joist, and joists.

Hoist It Out of the Way

There are several methods available for stowing bulky items like bikes or ladders in the garage. There are simple ceiling hooks and wall hooks, overhead racks for ladders, and even a "claw" for bikes. You screw the claw to the ceiling and it grabs the rim when you bump a wheel against it.

A hoist is a convenient way to get moderately heavy stuff up out of the way without having to muscle it over your head. You'll find hoists designed for bikes and very similar systems designed for ladders, kayaks, or canoes.

GARDEN TOOL RACK

In less than an hour, you can get that jumble of long-handled yard tools neatly stored in this simple rack. The best part is the rack will be customized to exactly the tools you want to store. You can place it at any convenient height, as long as there is enough room for the tool handles to hang below. All you need is a length of 1×6 lumber, two 5-in. by 6-in. metal brackets, six 1¼-in. screws, and two ⅝-in. screws.

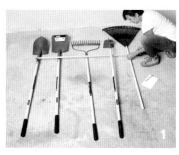

1. DECIDE ON THE LENGTH. Lay your long-handled garden tools side by side with about 2 in. clearance separating each tool from the next. Measuring across the point where the handle meets each tool, determine the distance from the middle of one handle to the middle of the next and write down these measurements.

2. CUT THE RACK TO LENGTH AND LAY OUT THE HOLES. Add 12 in. to the sum of your handle measurements and cut a 1×6 to that length. Use a combination square to draw a line along the length of the board, ¾ in. from one edge. Mark 6 in. along that line for the first tool and then make marks for the rest of the tool handles, adding 6 in. to each measurement you noted.

3. DRILL THE TOOL HOLES. Clamp the board to your bench with at least 2 in. overhanging along the length. Center a 2-in. hole saw over each mark and drill a hole. The saw will overlap the edge of the board, creating a slot for the handles. If you want to paint or finish the rack board, now is the time to do it.

QUICK TIP When using a hole saw, drill just until the pilot bit comes through the other side. Then flip the board, put the pilot bit in the pilot hole, and finish the cut. You'll get a cleaner cut, and the waste piece won't get stuck in the hole saw.

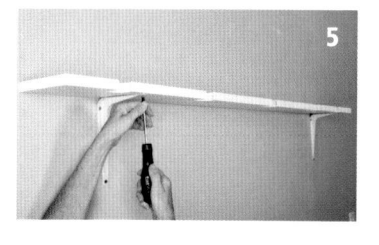

4. INSTALL THE BRACKETS. Use a 4-ft. level to draw a line on the wall at your chosen height. Find the two studs that fall closest to where you want the ends of your rack to be (see "Find the studs along the line" on p. 12). Center the brackets over the studs and with the line passing through the top holes of each bracket's long leg. Mark for the screw holes. Predrill and then attach the brackets with 1¼-in. screws.

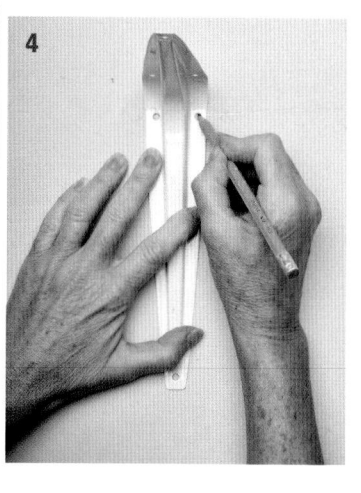

5. ATTACH THE RACK. Center the rack across the brackets, adjusting if necessary to prevent a slot from falling over a bracket. Mark for screw holes. Take the rack down to predrill and then secure it to the bracket with ⅝-in. screws.

FOLD-UP WORKTABLE/
TOOL CABINET

You long for a convenient workstation with a good-size table, a place with your tools and fasteners organized and right at hand. But you still need to get your car in the garage. Here's the solution. This project features a fold-up worktable with pegboard above and a cabinet below. Open the doors, slip on the removable feet, drop the table, and you have a rock-solid work surface. Close it up, and everything is hidden and protected in a unit that protrudes just 7 in. from the wall.

This worktable/tool cabinet is built from AC plywood. Use the clear "A" side for the faces of the doors and the work surface of the table. The shelves and trim pieces are #2 pine, which has some knots. The worktable is protected with two coats of wipe-on polyurethane.

Front View

Table and doors not shown

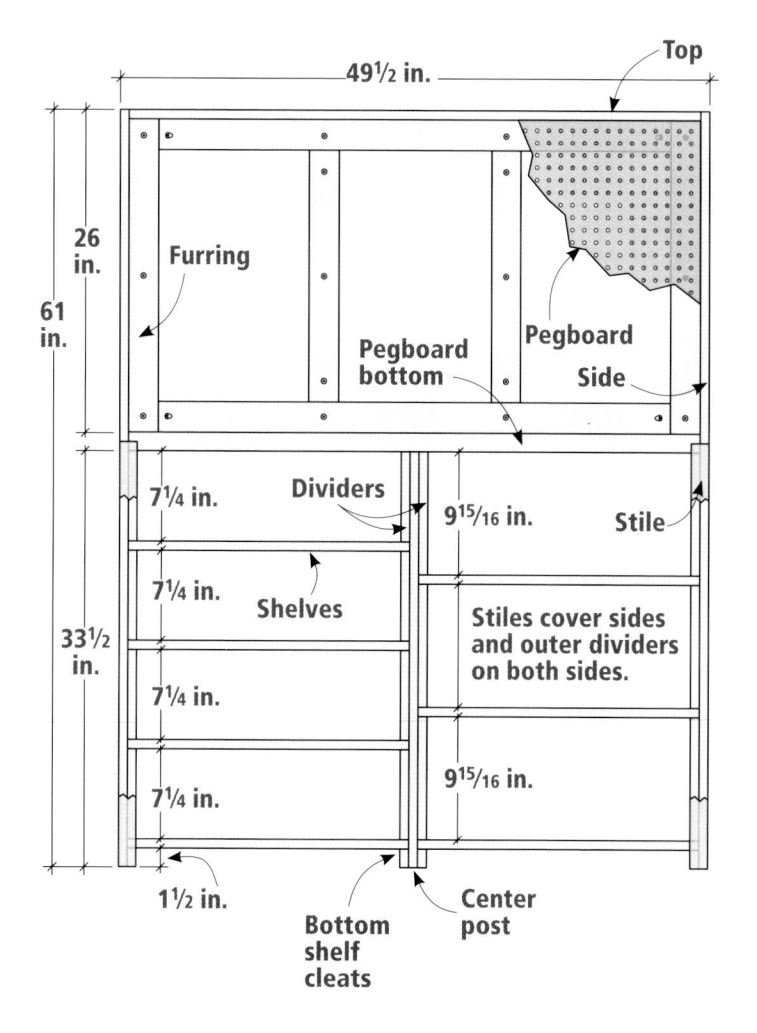

Top

49½ in.

26 in.

61 in.

Furring

Pegboard bottom

Pegboard Side

7¼ in.

Dividers

9¹⁵/₁₆ in.

Stile

7¼ in.

Shelves

Stiles cover sides and outer dividers on both sides.

33½ in.

7¼ in.

7¼ in.

9¹⁵/₁₆ in.

1½ in.

Bottom shelf cleats

Center post

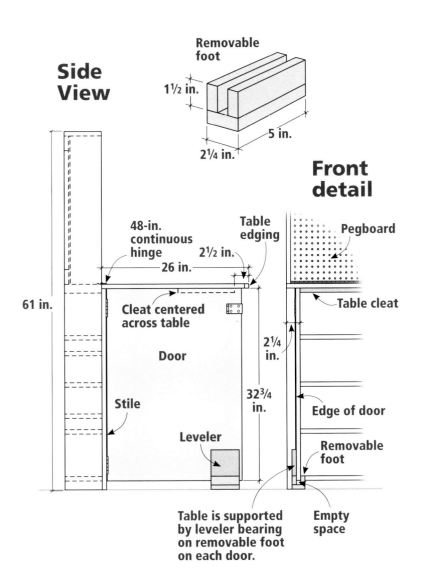

Side View

Removable foot

1½ in.

5 in.

2¼ in.

Front detail

48-in. continuous hinge

Table edging

2½ in.

26 in.

Pegboard

61 in.

Cleat centered across table

Table cleat

2¼ in.

Door

32¾ in.

Stile

Leveler

Edge of door

Removable foot

Table is supported by leveler bearing on removable foot on each door.

Empty space

WHAT YOU'LL NEED

- 2 side furring   ¾ in. × 2½ in. × 25¼ in., pine
- 2 top and bottom furring   ¾ in. × 2½ in. × 43 in., pine
- 2 middle furring   ¾ in. × 2½ in. × 20¼ in., pine
- 1 pegboard   25¼ in. × 48 in.
- 2 sides   ¾ in. × 5½ in. × 61 in., pine
- 1 top   ¾ in. × 5½ in. × 48 in., pine
- 1 pegboard bottom   1½ in. × 5½ in. × 48 in., pine
- 1 center post   ¾ in. × 5½ in. × 33½ in., pine
- 7 shelves   ¾ in. × 5½ in. × 23⅝ in., pine
- 8 dividers   ¾ in. × 5½ in. × 7¼ in., pine
- 6 dividers   ¾ in. × 5½ in. × 9¹⁵⁄₁₆ in., pine
- 4 bottom shelf cleats   ¾ in. × 5½ in. × 1½ in., pine
- 2 stiles   ¾ in. × 1½ in. × 34¼ in., pine
- 2 doors   ¾ in. × 23⅛ in. × 32¾ in., plywood
- 1 worktable   ¾ in. × 25¼ in. × 48 in., plywood
- 2 door foot bottoms   ¾ in. × 2¼ in. × 5 in., plywood
- 4 door foot sides   ¾ in. × 1½ in. × 5 in., plywood
- 2 levelers   ¾ in. × 5 in. × 5 in., plywood
- 2 side table edging   ¾ in. × ¾ in. × 25¼ in.
- 1 front table edging   ¾ in. × ¾ in. × 49½ in.
- 1 table cleat   ¾ in. × 10 in. × 45 in., plywood

HARDWARE

- 4 hinges   ¾ in. × 2½ in.
- 1 continuous hinge   48 in.
- 2 hooks and eyes   2½ in.
- 1 swivel hasp   4½ in.
- 1¼-in. screws
- 1½-in. screws
- 2½-in. screws
- 4d finish nails
- 8d finish nails

INSTALL THE PEGBOARD AND FRAME

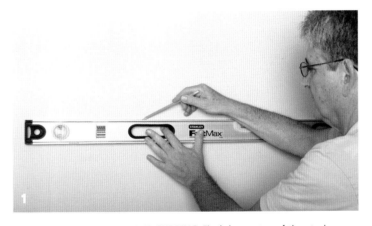

1. LOCATE THE PEGBOARD AND FURRING. Find the center of the stud near-est to where you want to locate the left side of the pegboard (see "Find the studs along the line" on p. 12). Then find the centers of the next three studs to the right. To locate the left side of the pegboard, measure 1¼ in. to the left of the center of the stud. Use a 4-ft. level to make a plumb line from the floor up to 60¼ in. Draw another plumb line 48 in. to the right to locate the right side of the pegboard. Connect the top of the lines with a level line for the top of the pegboard.

2. CUT AND ATTACH THE FURRING.

The pegboard is "furred out" from the wall to allow room for the tool hangers. Cut the outside furring strips to the dimensions in the parts list, then attach them with 2½-in. screws. Next, cut and install the horizontal furring strips with 2½-in. screws every 6 in. into studs. To catch the studs, toe-screw the horizontal strips into the side vertical strips as shown. Finally, cut and install two middle vertical strips centered over the studs.

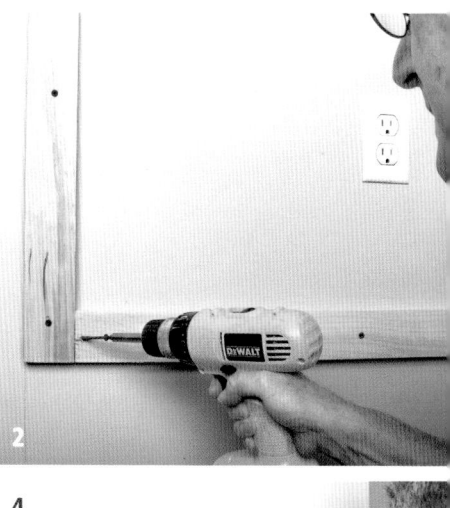

3. CUT THE PEGBOARD. Use a circular saw with a jig to crosscut the pegboard to 25¼ in. Put the pegboard on the floor with a sacrificial piece of plywood underneath and lay out a crosscut at 25¼ in. Set the blade on your circular saw to cut through the pegboard and into the sacrificial piece without cutting into the floor.

4. INSTALL THE PEGBOARD. Attach the pegboard to the furring strips with 1¼-in. screws into the corners and every six holes along the perimeter and the middle strips.

Make a Crosscutting Jig for a Circular Saw

Start with a piece of ¼-in. plywood base that's 48 in. long and at least 6 in. wider than the base of your saw. Glue and clamp a ¾-in. by 6-in. by 52-in. plywood guide flush to the outside edge of the base and overhanging about 2 in. on each side. When the glue dries, clamp the jig to your bench with enough of the base overhanging so that you can run your circular saw along the guide, trimming the base. To use the jig, clamp or screw it to the sacrificial piece with the trimmed edge of the jig base at the cutline on the workpiece.

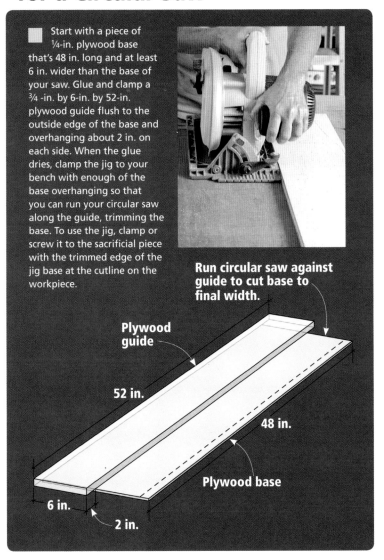

Run circular saw against guide to cut base to final width.

Plywood guide

52 in.

48 in.

Plywood base

6 in.

2 in.

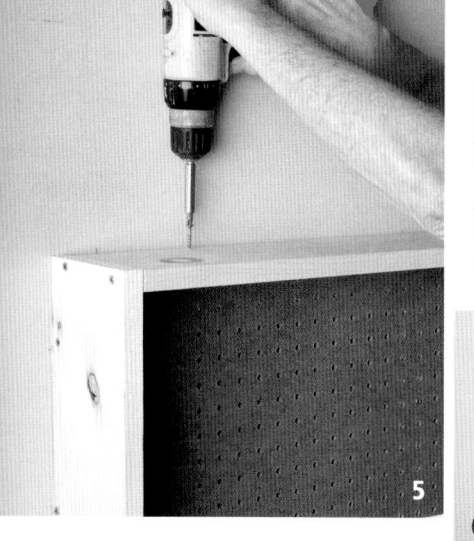

5. CUT AND INSTALL THE SIDES AND TOP.
Cut the sides to the dimensions in the parts list. Attach them to the side furring strips with 1¼-in. screws. Cut the top to fit between the sides and attach it with two screws through each side and screws down into the furring.

6. CUT AND ATTACH THE 2×6 PEGBOARD BOTTOM.
Cut a piece of 2×6 to 48 in. With a helper holding it in place, attach the piece with 2½-in. screws up into the furring and then drive two screws through each side.

Extend an Outlet

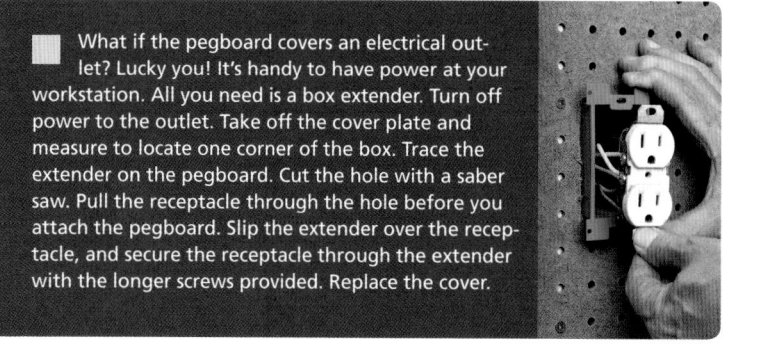

What if the pegboard covers an electrical outlet? Lucky you! It's handy to have power at your workstation. All you need is a box extender. Turn off power to the outlet. Take off the cover plate and measure to locate one corner of the box. Trace the extender on the pegboard. Cut the hole with a saber saw. Pull the receptacle through the hole before you attach the pegboard. Slip the extender over the receptacle, and secure the receptacle through the extender with the longer screws provided. Replace the cover.

INSTALL THE SHELVES

The 1×6 shelves will butt into each side of the cabinet and the center post and will be positioned and supported by the 1×6 dividers. Cut the center post to fit between the 2×6 pegboard bottom and the floor. Cut the seven shelves, the eight left-hand dividers, and the six right-hand dividers to the lengths in the parts list. For quick accuracy, make the cuts using stops on a power miter saw. Otherwise, a circular saw will do fine.

1. INSTALL THE CENTER POST. Put two shelves up against the bottom of the 2×6 with the center post fitted between. This will position the center post while you secure it with two 2½-in. screws through the 2×6. Then remove the shelves.

2. INSTALL THE LEFT-HAND SHELVES AND DIVIDERS. Install a pair of short dividers with four 1¼-in. screws, clamp a shelf in place, and secure it with two 2¼-in. screws on each end. Repeat for all four left-hand shelves and their dividers. Extend lines around the outside of the cabinet as you go to ensure that your screws don't miss the shelves.

3. INSTALL THE RIGHT-HAND SHELVES. Install the top two right-hand shelves and their dividers as you did on the left, but this time use 2½-in. screws through the left-hand dividers and the center post into the shelves.

4. INSTALL THE FINAL SHELF. You won't have access to the inside end of the last shelf, so predrill holes for toe-screws into the divider and secure with 1½-in. screws as shown.

5. CUT AND INSTALL THE BOTTOM SHELF CLEATS. For both ends of both bottom shelves, scribe cuts on pieces of 1×6 to fit snugly underneath. Cut the pieces and tap them into place with a hammer. No need for fasteners or glue.

6. CUT AND INSTALL THE STILES. Rip pine to 1½ in. wide for the stiles and cut them to reach from the floor to ¾ in. below the top of the 2×6. Install them with glue and 8d finish nails.

MAKE AND INSTALL THE DOORS AND WORKTABLE

1. CUT THE DOORS AND WORKTABLE. Check your door dimensions—they may vary a bit from the dimensions in the parts list. For the height of the doors, measure from the bottom of the shelves to the top of the stiles. For the width, measure between the inside of the stiles, divide in half, and subtract 1/16 in. for each door. Using the same technique as for the pegboard, crosscut a plywood sheet to the door height. Then rip the doors to final width on the tablesaw or with the circular saw and jig. Use the circular saw and jig to crosscut the worktable to 25¼ in.

2. MARK THE HINGE LOCATIONS. On the face of the doors, mark hinge locations 2 in. from the top and bottom. Put each door in position and shim it flush to the top of the stiles. Then transfer the hinge locations onto the stiles.

3. SCRIBE THE MORTISES. Scribe the outline of each hinge mortise on the outside edge of each door and the inside of the stiles. Set a combination square to the thickness of a hinge leaf and use it to scribe the mortise depth on the faces of the stiles and doors.

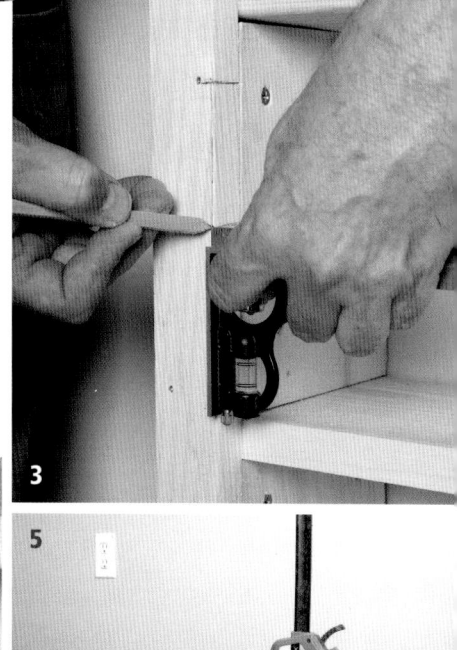

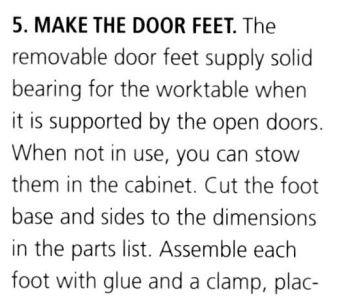

4. CUT THE MORTISES AND INSTALL THE DOORS. Chop the sides of the mortises and then slice them out to depth. Attach the hinges to the doors and then to the stiles.

> **QUICK TIP** When chopping mortises, place the chisel on the scribe line with the flat side toward the outside of the mortise. Tap the chisel with a mallet or hammer until it cuts to the scribed hinge depth.

5. MAKE THE DOOR FEET. The removable door feet supply solid bearing for the worktable when it is supported by the open doors. When not in use, you can stow them in the cabinet. Cut the foot base and sides to the dimensions in the parts list. Assemble each foot with glue and a clamp, placing the sides flush to the edges of the base.

Stanley garage storage solutions

in from the outside edge. Open a door until it is perpendicular to the 2×6—use a framing square to check. Put a foot in place, put glue on the back of the leveler, and push the edge of the leveler firmly against the foot as you clamp the leveler in place. Now, even if your garage floor isn't level, the door feet will fit snugly under the levelers, firmly supporting the worktable.

7. INSTALL THE TABLE EDGING. Use a utility knife and square to scribe cuts in place as shown. First, cut the side edging pieces so that they will fit flush with the front and back of the worktable. Install the pieces with glue and 4d finish nails. Cut the front edging to cover the ends of the side edging and install with glue and nails.

QUICK TIP It's a good idea to protect the working surface of the worktable with a couple of coats of polyurethane. You can brush it on or, easier, use the wipe-on variety.

8. INSTALL THE CONTINUOUS HINGE. Put the tabletop in place on the open doors with feet in place. Center the continuous hinge over where the tabletop abuts the 2×6 pegboard bottom. Predrill and screw the hinge in place.